Arrow Book of
Presidents

by STURGES F. CARY

illustrated by Leo Summers
and Ted Hanke

SCHOLASTIC BOOK SERVICES
NEW YORK • TORONTO • LONDON • AUCKLAND • SYDNEY • TOKYO

Contents

Engravings courtesy of U.S. Bureau of Engraving and Printing

Cover photo: Dennis Brack/Black Star © 1979

ISBN: 0-590-31805-5

Copyright © 1980, 1976, 1972, 1966, 1965 by Scholastic Magazines, Inc. All rights reserved. Published by Scholastic Book Services, a Division of Scholastic Magazines, Inc.

12 11 10 9 8 7 6 5 4 3 2 1   9   0 1 2 3 4 5/8

Printed in the U.S.A.   01

How the Presidency Began

IN 1775, kings ruled in nearly every country in the world — even in America. The 13 American colonies were ruled by George III of England. After the War of Independence, the colonies became the United States of America, free to set up their own kind of government.

They wanted a government that represented the will of the people, not a king's will; they decided to choose a *President* to head the government. Every four years, the nation would have a chance to choose another President. There have been Presidential elections every four years since 1788.

Who Can Be President

The Constitution says the President must be at least 35 years old, must have lived in the United States for 14 years, and must be a United States citizen from birth. (A naturalized citizen cannot become President.)

A man or woman with these three qualifications may serve as President.

How Parties Choose the Candidates

To be elected President, a person must have the support of a strong political party.

There were no political parties when our nation began. But very soon, differences of opinion arose about how to run the government. Political leaders separated into two main groups — the Federalist Party and the Democratic-Republican Party — each with its own ideas about how to govern the country.

Since then, we have almost always had two strong political parties. Their names have changed through the years. Today we have the Republican Party and the Democratic Party, and most voters are either Republicans or Democrats.

Every four years each political party holds its national convention where party leaders from all the states meet to choose their party's candidate for President and Vice-President (the person who will become President should the President die in office).

Usually several small parties have candidates for President, too, but none of these candidates has ever been elected. Small parties are often important. They give people a chance to express opinions or ideas that are not put forth by the two main parties.

Electing the President

On Election Day the people vote for the candidate of their choice. This "popular vote"—the vote of the people—is counted. That leads to the next step—figuring up the "electoral vote," state by state.

Every state has a certain number of electoral votes. The states with fewest people—now Alaska, Delaware, Nevada, North Dakota, Vermont, Wyoming — have three electoral votes each. So has the District of Columbia. Other states have more, depending on their population. New York now has 41 electoral votes; California has 45. They are the states with the most people.

On Election Day, the candidate who gets the most popular votes in a state gets *all* that state's electoral votes. In 1976, for example, 3,882,244 Californians voted for the Republican candidate, 742,284 for the Democratic, and nearly a quarter of a million for other candidates. So the Republican candidate got all of California's 45 electoral votes.

Soon after Election Day, the electoral vote can be added up. The Republican candidate for President gets the electoral votes of the states in which he won the popular vote. The Democratic candidate gets the electoral votes of the states in which *he* won. Sometimes the candidate of a small party gets a few electoral votes. There are 538 electoral votes, equal to the number of Senators and Representatives the states send to Congress. The candidate who gets more than half these votes wins. If no candidate gets a majority, the House of Representatives chooses the President from the three candidates who have the most electoral votes.

Inauguration Day

At noon on the January 20 following Election Day, the President-Elect stands on the Capitol steps in Washington, D.C., and takes the Oath of Office. This is the Inauguration ceremony. At the moment he takes the oath he becomes the President of the United States.

Oath of Office

"I do solemnly swear (or affirm) that I will faithfully execute the Office of President of the United States, and will to the best of my ability, preserve, protect and defend the Constitution of the United States."

—from Article II, Section 1, U.S. Constitution

The President's Duties

The President holds the highest public office in the United States. His duty is to lead our nation according to our Constitution and our laws, which are made by Congress. Often he presents to Congress his ideas for new laws which are needed. The President is the head of his political party, but his duty is to work for all the people.

As head of the United States, the President is the Commander-in-Chief of our Army, Navy, and Air Force. He speaks for our country in its dealings with foreign nations. He appoints many public officials.

The President also has charge of the work of about three million U.S. Government employees.

The Cabinet

Helping him in this task are the heads of the 13 executive departments of the government. These 13 officials are often called in by the President to give him advice on the country's problems. When they meet as a group, they are known as the Cabinet.

Cabinet Offices

Secretary of State

Secretary of the
Treasury

Secretary of Defense

Attorney General

Secretary of the
Interior

Secretary of
Agriculture

Secretary of Commerce

Secretary of Labor

Secretary of Health
and Human Services

Secretary of Education

Secretary of Housing
and Urban
Development

Secretary of
Transportation

Secretary of Energy

There are also several Executive Agencies
that include the National Security Council, the
Central Intelligence Agency (C.I.A.), and others.

In addition, there is a White House staff that
includes the Chief of Staff, Press Secretary, and a
number of Presidential Assistants.

Our first President's first Inauguration took place at Federal Hall in New York City, which was then the nation's capital.

George Washington

Born: February 22, 1732
Died: December 14, 1799
Years in office: April 30, 1789 — March 3, 1797

He might have been King George instead of President Washington. Some people wanted George Washington to make himself king of America. But he had fought through the long Revolutionary War to free America from the rule of England's king and he wanted no kings in America.

It seemed natural for people to want Washington as their chief. From his youth, he had been a leader of men — as a boy of the frontier, fearless and at home in the woods; then as a soldier in the French and Indian War. He looked like a leader, too — six feet two inches tall, and handsome.

In 1775 the American colonies made the great decision: they must fight against England's rule. When our war for independence began, George Washington was asked to lead the American troops. In the eight years of the Revolutionary War, Washington lost more battles than he won and he retreated more often than he advanced. But he held his poorly trained army together through days of hunger and defeat, and he led them to victory.

After the war, Washington returned to Mount Vernon, his beautiful home beside the Potomac River. But he could not retire — not yet! The 13 states, united in war, were quarreling about the kind of government that they needed as a nation. In 1787 a meeting was held to work out these problems. George Washington, as a leader respected by all, was asked to preside at this meeting. Out of this convention came the Constitution, which set up our form of government and created the office of President.

Who should be the first President? Nearly everyone agreed: George Washington. President Washington then chose the best men he knew to help him. Thomas Jefferson was his Secretary of State, and Alexander Hamilton his Secretary of the Treasury.

President Washington served one four-year

term and then another. During his Presidency the young United States grew to 16 states. The new government had a good start. Washington did not want to serve a third term. He was 64 years old, and he was tired.

Washington's last years at Mount Vernon were happy ones. He had always loved dancing and horse races and fox hunting and big parties. Now he could relax and do what he wanted. Each day he was up and off on horseback to see what

In 1793 Eli Whitney invented the cotton gin, a machine which made it easy to separate cotton fibers from the seeds. Cotton became the South's chief crop, and slavery grew.

was going on around the farm. Guests often gathered at his table in the evenings. His wife, Martha, saw to it that they left by nine o'clock, for that was General Washington's bedtime!

While he was President, Washington helped choose the very place — not far from Mount Vernon — where the nation's new capital city was to stand. It was named for him: Washington, D.C. The state of Washington was named in his honor, too — and all over our land there are cities and lakes and mountains and islands that also bear his name.

Mount Vernon was a typical Southern plantation. You can see it today, much as it looked when the Washington family lived there.

John Adams

Born: October 30, 1735
Died: July 4, 1826
Years in office: March 4, 1797 — March 3, 1801
Party: Federalist

When you watch fireworks on July Fourth, think of John Adams. For Independence Day, he said, should be celebrated "with... games ... bells ... bonfires ... from this time forward...."

Adams was one of the first men to argue that America should seek freedom from English rule. Not many agreed with him at first, but gradually more and more people decided he was right.

John Adams served with Thomas Jefferson on the committee that wrote the Declaration of Independence. He helped convince the Continental Congress — our first American government — that the Declaration should be accepted. And so on July 4, 1776, our nation was born.

Some of the causes for which Adams fought,

such as independence, were unpopular at the time. Just before the Revolutionary War, some British soldiers fired into a crowd in Boston, Massachusetts, and were arrested. Adams believed every man was entitled to a fair trial. When no one else would help the soldiers, he acted as their lawyer.

While Adams was President, France attacked some of our ships. Many people demanded war against France, but Adams didn't believe we should fight. Though some people called him a traitor, he kept war from breaking out.

John Adams was the first President to live

Adams kept us out of a war with France when that country's ships fired on, and seized, ships of the new United States.

in the new capital city of Washington, D.C. When he arrived, half-finished buildings stood in the midst of swamp and forest. Streets were unpaved. In the White House — then called the "President's House" — only six rooms were ready. Mrs. Adams hung her washing in the empty East Room!

John Adams lived to see his son, John Quincy Adams, become President. This has been the only father-son pair of Presidents in our history. Many men in the Adams family later became leaders of our nation — Cabinet members, ambassadors, writers. No member of this great family was more respected than that stubborn, honest old fighter for freedom, John Adams.

Thomas Jefferson

Born: April 13, 1743
Died: July 4, 1826
Years in office: March 4, 1801 — March 3, 1809
Party: Democratic-Republican

Thomas Jefferson was interested in almost everything there was to learn.

Science fascinated him. He had his own museum. Among the fossils he collected was the jawbone of a mammoth — a prehistoric elephant. Jefferson collected books, too. His personal library contained ten thousand books — one of the biggest collections of his time.

Jefferson was a master of his own language, but he knew Italian, Spanish, French, Irish, Latin, and Greek as well.

He was a famous architect. He designed and built his own home on a little mountain in Virginia. He named the house "Monticello," which means "little mountain" in Italian.

Thomas Jefferson loved gadgets. At Monticello you can see the clock he built, run by cannon balls as weights; and a contraption he designed to make several copies of a letter at one time.

Jefferson was a scientific farmer. He invented a new kind of plow, and was one of the first farmers in America to use farm machinery.

Thomas Jefferson was interested in everything and he was good at everything he tried. But there were three things above all that he was proud of. You can read about them in the words

Thomas Jefferson designed and built Monticello. And he filled it with many of his clever inventions.

he himself wrote for the stone over his grave: "Here lies Thomas Jefferson, author of the Declaration of American Independence, of the Statute of Virginia for Religious Freedom, and father of the University of Virginia."

Though it isn't mentioned on his gravestone, Jefferson held just about every important public office, from governor to President. He made the "Louisiana Purchase," whereby the United States bought from France the Louisiana Territory — the land around the Mississippi and Missouri rivers. It doubled the size of our country.

He also ordered the Lewis and Clark expedition to explore the unknown land of what is now northwest U.S.

Jefferson was tall and bony, with freckles and red hair. Fashionable gentlemen in those days hid their hair under white wigs, but not Jefferson. He even thought it too grand to ride in a coach to his Inauguration. He just stepped out of his boardinghouse and walked over to the Capitol building with his friends. It was one way Thomas Jefferson had of showing his belief that, as he wrote in the Declaration of Independence, "all men are created equal."

James Madison

Born: March 16, 1751
Died: June 28, 1836
Years in office: March 4, 1809 — March 3, 1817
Party: Democratic-Republican

After Jefferson, who was one of our tallest Presidents, came the shortest. "Little Jemmy" Madison stood only five feet four. At his Inauguration as President, it was hard to see him in the crowd. No one could miss his wife, though; the ostrich feather in Dolley Madison's hat waved high above everything.

Dolley was 17 years younger than her shy, gentle husband, and was the gayest party-giver in Washington. At her parties many people had their first taste of a new dessert called "ice cream."

James Madison seemed out of place at his wife's lively parties. Even as a boy he would rather read than play. Later, at Princeton College, he was too busy to be sociable. By studying hard and sleeping only three hours a night, he finished two years of college in one year.

Some people thought Madison was out of place not only at parties but as a wartime President, too. "Mr. Madison's War" — that's what his enemies called the War of 1812 while he was President. This war was almost a disaster for the

People laughed at "Fulton's folly" — until they saw Robert Fulton's *Clermont* steam up the Hudson River in 1807. Soon hundreds of steamboats were at work on our rivers and lakes.

United States. The British captured the city of Washington and set fire to the White House.

The War of 1812 was not very glorious, but it helped to knit our new nation together. After his eight weary years in office, Madison gladly returned home to Virginia.

Long before James Madison became President, he played an important part in forming our national government. After the Revolutionary War, the states began quarreling among themselves. Madison felt that we needed a strong national government in order to survive. More than any other man, he created our Constitution.

Madison also fought for the first ten amendments to the Constitution, which became the "Bill of Rights." These amendments protect such liberties as freedom of speech, freedom of the press, freedom of religion, the right to have a trial by jury if you are accused of a crime, and the right to meet and complain about an unfair law.

Madison himself wrote nine of these amendments. For these rights that he helped to bring to all Americans, he will always be remembered.

James Monroe

Born: April 28, 1758

Died: July 4, 1831

Years in office: March 4, 1817 — March 3, 1825

Party: Democratic-Republican

Like three Presidents before him, James Monroe came from Virginia. His two homes — first Ash Lawn, later Oak Hill — were less than 100 miles away from Washington's Mount Vernon, Jefferson's Monticello, and Madison's Montpelier.

The four neighbors were more than just friends. They had worked together for this country from the days of the Revolutionary War. Monroe was only 18 years old when he was wounded in that war. Soon after, Washington promoted Monroe to captain for his bravery.

As a boy, James Monroe used to walk to school through the deep woods, with his gun under one arm and his books under the other. He kept his family supplied with rabbits and squirrels that he shot on the way home.

"Try, try again" might have been Monroe's motto. He was not discouraged even when he made mistakes. And finally he won the prize he wanted most: the Presidency.

To young Americans born after the Revolutionary War, President Monroe seemed like the last of the old heroes. He looked the part, too

Wagonloads of settlers bumped westward on the National Pike. It was the first hard-surfaced road over the mountains to Ohio.

— tall and dignified, and a little old-fashioned. Long after most people had given up the old styles of clothing, he still wore knee breeches, shoes with buckles, and a three-cornered hat.

Monroe was so popular as President that when he ran for a second term, nobody ran against him. The nation was growing fast. It was a time of peace. People called these years "the era of good feeling."

The good feeling reached out to our Latin-American neighbors, too. These new nations, encouraged by our revolution against England, rebelled against their rulers in Spain. President Monroe backed them up. He gave this warning to Spain and other European nations: "Keep hands off North and South America." We remember James Monroe for this "Monroe Doctrine."

John Quincy Adams

Born: July 11, 1767

Died: February 23, 1848

Years in office: March 4, 1825 — March 3, 1829

Party: Democratic-Republican

At Quincy, Massachusetts, two Presidents are buried side by side: the Adamses, father and son. They had been born in houses that stood next to each other on the same land. They both went to Harvard College, became lawyers, lived in the same house in their later years. Both were short and bald and stubborn as mules.

Both helped to write peace treaties to end wars with England — John Adams after the Revolutionary War, and John Quincy Adams after the War of 1812. Each served only one term as President the anted a second term. Both lived to fact, John Quincy Adams lived to see the invented. He is the first President whose paph exists.

Some Presidents retire quietly when they

The Erie Canal, completed in 1825, joined New York City and the Great Lakes. Horses pulled the barges up and down the canal.

leave the White House. Not John Quincy Adams! He was the only former President to be elected to the House of Representatives. Some people said it was not dignified for a President to take a lower job. But John Quincy Adams did not worry about whether it was dignified or not. He thought that being a Congressman was another chance to serve his country.

The country's most argued topic then was what to do about the slaves in America. Our

Southern states wanted to keep their slaves. But men like John Quincy Adams believed that all men should be free. In Congress he argued against having slaves. He brought in petitions asking for an end to slavery. Other Congressmen were annoyed. They didn't want to hear about this touchy subject, and they tried to silence the noisy old man.

John Quincy Adams kept talking. He convinced many people that slavery was wrong, but he never lived to see the Civil War which brought an end to slavery. One day in 1848, as he waited for a chance to speak in the House of Representatives, he collapsed from a stroke. Two days later he died — a fighter to the end.

Andrew Jackson

Born: March 15, 1767
Died: June 8, 1845
Years in office: March 4, 1829 — March 3, 1837
Party: Democratic

A boyhood friend said Andy Jackson was "the most roaring, rollicking, horse-racing, card-playing, mischievous fellow" in town.

People either loved this terrible-tempered redhead or they hated him. Jackson was such a strong President that his enemies called him "King Andrew." John Quincy Adams said he was a "barbarian." In the War of 1812, Jackson's fellow soldiers nicknamed him "Old Hickory," because hickory was the toughest wood they knew.

It is true that Andrew Jackson was a rough-and-ready fellow. He had been so nearly all his life. When he was 13 years old, he fought in the Revolution. He was captured and ordered to clean a British officer's boots, but he refused. The officer drew his sword and struck Andrew across the arm and head. Andrew still wouldn't clean the boots.

At the age of 14, Andrew became an orphan. By 21 he was one of the few lawyers in the wilds of west Tennessee, always getting into fist fights and duels. With men like Sam Houston and Davy Crockett, he fought fierce wars against the Indians.

In the War of 1812, British soldiers marched on the city of New Orleans. "Old Hickory" and his riflemen were waiting. From behind a mud wall just south of the city, they mowed down the British troops. The most tragic part of this battle is that the war was already over, but neither side

Cyrus McCormick's reaper cut grain much faster than men could do it by hand. This first step in replacing farm labor with machinery made possible the great Midwest wheat farms.

Snorting along its tracks came the fabulous "iron horse." This railway engine, one of the first, ran in New York in 1831.

knew it. A peace treaty had been signed in Europe. The news hadn't yet reached America.

Jackson's victory at New Orleans made him a hero. From then on, people began thinking of him as a future President.

The plain people liked Jackson. When he won the Presidency in 1828, farmers, workmen, and frontiersmen hurried to Washington. After his Inauguration, cheering crowds stormed into the White House. They stood with muddy boots on satin-covered chairs, smashed dishes, and trampled food into the rugs, shouting for joy. Yet it was not a happy time for Jackson. His wife Rachel had died a few months earlier, and victory did not seem sweet.

Andrew Jackson said, "Let the people rule." To him, this meant putting his own followers into public office. He fired a thousand government workers and put members of his own party in their jobs.

Until Jackson's time, candidates for President were chosen by Congress. Congressmen from each party would meet to choose their party's candidate for President. In 1832 the Democrats tried something new. They held a national convention to renominate Jackson as their candidate. Ever since, our Presidents have been nominated at party conventions made up of delegates from every state.

Andrew Jackson was a Southerner, but when the Southern state of South Carolina threatened to leave the Union, Jackson said this must not happen. At a dinner party, he rose to give a toast. Looking directly at the South Carolina leaders, he said, "Our Union — it must be preserved!" Jackson believed that our nation was one and indivisible. Thirty years later we would fight a Civil War for that same belief.

Martin Van Buren

Born: December 5, 1782

Died: July 24, 1862

Years in office: March 4, 1837 — March 3, 1841

Party: Democratic

Our first seven Presidents had been born in Colonial America. Martin Van Buren, the eighth President, was born in the new United States of America.

"Mat" Van Buren was a friendly man, always ready with a smile, a handshake, and a joke. It was easy to like this cheerful, well-dressed fellow with the fancy sideburn whiskers.

One of the men who liked him most was Andrew Jackson. Van Buren worked hard to help Jackson become President in 1828. In return, Jackson made him Secretary of State. He also saw to it that Van Buren ran successfully for Vice President. Then in 1836, Van Buren ran for President. Jackson supported him, and that was enough to get Van Buren elected.

But "Little Van's" popularity did not last long. Hard times had come. All over the country, banks closed and people lost their money. Factories closed and workers lost their jobs. Many people thought the President should do something about this. But Van Buren did little because he believed businessmen should settle their own problems.

Van Buren's failure to act made him unpopular with people who did not have jobs or

In Van Buren's time there was no secret ballot. Voters made their choices by voice vote or signed ballot. Election Day was full of excitement.

enough food. Stories spread about the gold dinner plates he ate from at the White House, and the big olive-colored coach he rode in, and the way his daughter-in-law sat like a queen on a platform during White House parties.

No wonder Martin Van Buren wasn't re-elected! But he welcomed the new President to the White House and became the first defeated candidate to help his rival get a smooth start in office.

In 1844 Van Buren again wanted to be the Democratic candidate for President, but he was not nominated. In 1848, however, he was nominated by the Free Soil Party — a new party which opposed slavery — but he did not win. After that, he did not try again.

William Henry Harrison

Born: February 9, 1773
Died: April 4, 1841
Years in office: March 4, 1841 — April 4, 1841
Party: Whig

We changed Presidents more often in the 25 years before the Civil War than at any other time in our history. Between Jackson and Lincoln, eight Presidents came and went. None served more than a single four-year term. Unluckiest of all was William Henry Harrison, who was President just 32 days. He never had a chance to show what kind of President he could be.

People did know that Harrison was a brave soldier. That was the main reason they elected him. One of General Harrison's most famous deeds had been to defeat the Shawnee Indians at Tippecanoe Creek, Indiana, in 1811. He had also been a hero in the War of 1812.

Years later, when the Whig political party

was looking for a popular man to run for President, they remembered "Old Tippecanoe." They made sure the people would remember him too. They coined this slogan: "Tippecanoe and Tyler Too!" (Tyler was the candidate for Vice President.) It was one of the noisiest campaigns we ever had. All across the country the Whigs shouted their slogan at meetings and parades and rallies. At night there were parades by torchlight. Harrison won. He was now 68 — the oldest man to be inaugurated as President.

Inauguration Day was cold and stormy, but Harrison wouldn't wear a coat or hat. He rode for two hours on horseback in a parade. He made a two-hour speech in the open air. That night the new President went to three Inaugural Balls — parties in his honor.

The excitement and the weather were too much for "Old Tippecanoe." He caught a cold, which grew worse after he went shopping for vegetables one chilly March morning. Harrison died on April 4, 1841, the first President to die in office.

John Tyler

Born: March 29, 1790
Died: January 18, 1862
Years in office: April 6, 1841 — March 3, 1845
Party: Whig

No one dreamed that Vice President John Tyler would become President. All Vice Presidents before him had served out their terms with little to do. Then President Harrison died. The Constitution says that in such a situation the Vice President takes over the duties of the President. At once, questions arose. What title should Tyler be given? Was he still Vice President? What new powers, if any, did he have?

Cabinet members suggested he be called "Vice President of the United States, acting President." But mild, softspoken John Tyler said no. He said he had become President. He said he had the full powers of the Presidency. Ever since then, whenever a President has died, the Vice

President has acted as John Tyler did and has taken over the Presidency.

Tyler's firmness was a shock to the Whig leaders. So were his political ideas. The Whigs wanted to increase taxes on imported goods, to set up a special bank for the government's

Samuel Morse invented the telegraph, and a dot-dash code. The first telegraph line went up between Washington and Baltimore.

money, to help the states build roads. Tyler opposed these plans. His whole Cabinet angrily resigned. Whig leaders declared that Tyler was no longer a member of their party.

In spite of these troubles, Tyler had some happy moments as President. One was his wedding day. He had been a widower for several years. While he was President, he married — the first President to be married in office. Another important day for Tyler was his very last one as President. All through his term of office he had wanted to see Texas become a state. On March 3, 1845, he signed a bill to make this possible.

In 1845 Tyler retired to his Virginia farm, "Sherwood Forest." He had named it after the woodland home of Robin Hood, the outlaw. Tyler said he felt like a "political outlaw," unwelcome in either the Whig or Democratic Party.

James Knox Polk

Born: November 2, 1795
Died: June 15, 1849
Years in office: March 4, 1845 — March 3, 1849
Party: Democratic

"I could not lose half a day just to go out and dine," growled James Knox Polk when he was invited to a party. His idea of life was work, work, work.

In college he was an honor student and never missed a class. In Congress he was fair and firm as Speaker of the House, and during fourteen years as a Congressman he was absent only once. Polk worked so hard for "Old Hickory" Andrew Jackson that people called him "Young Hickory."

In 1844 the Democrats could not decide, at first, on a candidate for President. Finally they agreed to nominate hard-working James K. Polk.

People called him a "dark-horse" candidate.

(At the race track a "dark horse" is a horse that nobody knows much about.) Polk ran against the famous Senator Henry Clay. On Election Day, Polk turned out to be the winner. At the age of 49 he became the youngest President elected up to that time.

During Polk's term of office, we fought a war with Mexico. Polk saw to it that in the peace treaty the United States was given all the land

Led by dreams of land and new homes, settlers crossed prairie and mountain on the Oregon Trail. The 2,000-mile trail began at Independence, Missouri. The trip took four to six months.

that is now California, Nevada, Utah, and much of Arizona, Colorado, New Mexico, and Wyoming. He helped fix the boundary between the United States and Canada. One historian has called him "one of the very best and most honest and most successful Presidents."

In the White House, the Polks lived simply. Mrs. Polk watched every penny. She did not allow dancing or card playing or alcoholic liquor or visitors on Sunday.

In his diary, President Polk wrote: "I am the hardest working man in the country." He worked so hard that he may have worn himself out. Three months after his term ended, he died.

Zachary Taylor

Born: November 24, 1784
Died: July 9, 1850
Years in office: March 5, 1849 — July 9, 1850
Party: Whig

Another Indian fighter, Zachary Taylor, galloped his way to the Presidency in 1848. General Taylor was dumpy, squint-eyed, and so short-legged that he couldn't mount a horse without help. Instead of a uniform, he sometimes wore his farm clothes and an old straw hat. But he could fight! He fought the Black Hawk and Seminole Indians along the frontier, and he fought the Mexicans too. During 40 years as a soldier, "Old Rough-and-Ready" Taylor never lost a battle.

Up to this time, the Whigs had elected only one President in the 16 years of their existence. He was the war hero "Old Tippecanoe" Harrison. Now the Whigs hoped they could win again with another famous soldier. They wanted Taylor for their candidate.

General Taylor wasn't interested. He had voted only once in his life. If he had any thoughts about how to run the country, he never mentioned them. The Whigs nominated Taylor just the same, and he won.

President Zachary Taylor was easygoing

The discovery of gold in California brought adventure-seekers from all over the world in the famous Gold Rush of 1849. Soon California had enough settlers to become a new U.S. state.

and friendly. He strolled around Washington, shaking hands with anyone he passed. He let Whitey, his faithful old war horse, graze on the White House lawn.

On July 4, 1850, President Taylor went to a celebration at the Washington Monument. It was a broiling-hot day, and the ceremony lasted for hours. Soon after Taylor returned home, he came down with a fever. Five days later he died. He had served only 16 months.

The Whig Party never elected another President.

Millard Fillmore

Born: January 7, 1800
Died: March 8, 1874
Years in office: July 10, 1850 — March 3, 1853
Party: Whig

Millard Fillmore's parents could hardly make a living from their poor farm in New York State. They sent Millard away to learn the clothmaker's trade when he was only 14 years old. The unhappy boy borrowed 30 dollars and paid it to his harsh master to let him go. Then he hiked 100 miles back to his log-cabin home.

For nine months a year, Fillmore worked in his father's stony fields. The other three months he went to Miss Abigail Powers' one-room school. With her encouragement, he bought himself a dictionary — the only book in the Fillmore home besides the family Bible. Miss Abigail, whom he married in 1826, also helped Fillmore become a lawyer.

Years later, as First Lady, Abigail Fillmore

was amazed to find no books at all in the White House. She fixed up one room as a library, and Congress provided 250 dollars to buy the books. She also had the first cookstove and water pipes put in the White House.

In the 1840's, slavery was our country's most serious problem. In the North, some people wanted to end slavery. The South wanted slavery to spread to new states in the West. Fillmore

The clipper ships were the fastest sailing ships of their day. The *Flying Cloud* raced from New York to San Francisco in 89 days.

didn't have strong opinions one way or the other. That is why the Whigs had picked him to run for Vice President with Zachary Taylor.

Then Taylor died and Fillmore became President. Congress passed the "Fugitive Slave Bill," which said that runaway slaves must be returned to their Southern masters. President Fillmore could kill this bill by refusing to sign it, or he could sign it and make it a law. He signed.

This turned out to be the biggest mistake of his life. All over the North people cried out against the cruel new law. The North never forgave Fillmore or his party. The Whigs lost so many members that the party just died away.

Franklin Pierce

Born: November 23, 1804
Died: October 8, 1869
Years in office: March 4, 1853 — March 3, 1857
Party: Democratic

This is the story of a man who had friends, success, popularity — and lost them all.

Smiling, handsome Franklin Pierce was a friend and college classmate of famous writers like Henry Wadsworth Longfellow and Nathaniel Hawthorne. He was a fine speaker and lawyer. He was elected to the New Hampshire state legislature when he was only 25 years old. At 29 he was in Congress. At 34 he was the youngest United States Senator. At 43 he was a general and a hero of the Mexican War. And at the age of 48 he became President. He might have been a happy man, but already things were starting to go wrong.

First came personal tragedies. Two of his sons died in babyhood. The third son was 11 years old when Pierce was elected President. As Mr. and Mrs. Pierce were getting ready to go to Washington for the Inauguration, a railroad car went off the track before their eyes and killed their boy. Mrs. Pierce had always been a shy woman. Now, grief-stricken, she lost interest in everything around her. From then on she dressed in black.

Pierce's term as President was tragic, too — for the nation as well as himself. He was a New Hampshire Yankee, but he seemed to go out of his way to help the Southerners who believed in slavery. The Northerners had a name for men like that: "Doughface."

Because Pierce insisted, Congress passed the Kansas-Nebraska Act. This law allowed slavery to spread because it let people in Kansas and Nebraska decide by a vote whether or not to have slavery. In Kansas, slave owners and enemies of slavery fought each other. "Bleeding Kansas" was a taste of the Civil War that was to tear our nation apart.

Pierce thought he was helping to hold the states together, but he left the Union more divided than ever. The Democrats would not renominate him. After a time, Pierce went back to New Hampshire and was soon a forgotten man.

James Buchanan

Born: April 23, 1791
Died: June 1, 1868
Years in office: March 4, 1857 — March 3, 1861
Party: Democratic

James Buchanan came into office with a shining record in private life and with much experience in public service. Buchanan first held public office when he was 23 years old. He earned 300,000 dollars as a lawyer before he was 30.

For 20 years "Old Buck" Buchanan had wanted to be President. When at last the honor came to him, he was too old and tired to do his best.

The Democratic Party was trying to dodge the question of slavery. The Democrats nominated Buchanan partly because he had been out of the country in the early 1850's. He had not taken part in the fierce arguments about slavery. As President, Buchanan would have to face up to the problem of slavery. But he didn't face up to it.

The first man to drill a well for oil was a railroad conductor named E. L. Drake. He struck oil in western Pennsylvania in 1859. This was the start of the oil industry in America.

Two days after Buchanan's Inauguration, the Supreme Court ruled that Congress had no power to interfere with slavery. Northerners were furious about this decision.

President Buchanan hoped the problem would go away if he did nothing about it. "You are sleeping on a volcano," he was warned. Still he couldn't decide what to do. The slave-owning Southern states threatened to secede — that is, to separate from the United States and form their own country. Buchanan said the Southern states had no lawful right to secede, but that the Northern states had no lawful right to stop them either.

In his last months as President, seven Southern states did leave the Union. They set themselves up as "The Confederate States of America" and chose Jefferson Davis as their President. Still Buchanan did nothing. He slipped away to his home in Pennsylvania and left the new President, Abraham Lincoln, to face the coming storm.

Abraham Lincoln

Born: February 12, 1809
Died: April 15, 1865
Years in office: March 4, 1861 — April 15, 1865
Party: Republican

"My father removed from Kentucky to Indiana in my tenth year. It was a wild region, with many bears and other wild animals still in the woods. There I grew up. There were some schools, so-called, but no qualification was ever required of a teacher beyond 'readin', writin', and cipherin'.' Of course, when I came of age I did not know much. ... I could read, write, and cipher, but that was all."

In telling this story of his early life, Abraham Lincoln left out one important detail: his fierce desire to learn. Others have told how he practiced writing by scratching letters on a wooden shovel with bits of charred wood, how he walked miles to borrow a book, and how he would read at night by the flickering firelight.

Lincoln's cousin, Dennis Hanks, once said, "I never seen Abe after he was 12 that he didn't have a book somewheres around." When he was older, Abe borrowed lawbooks and soon taught himself enough to be a lawyer.

In the growing town of Springfield, Illinois, his neighbors thought a lot of Abe Lincoln. They elected him to Congress. But they didn't re-elect him because he was against the Mexican War when most people were for it.

Lincoln quit politics. Soon he was making quite a lot of money as a lawyer. He could have been satisfied. But something kept gnawing at his conscience: slavery.

Lincoln had always hated slavery, but he did little about it until 1854. Then Congress passed the Kansas-Nebraska Act. It said that people in the Western territories could have slavery there if they voted to do so. Up and down the state of Illinois, Lincoln made speeches against this law.

The man who had written the Kansas-Nebraska Act was also from Springfield, Illinois. He was Senator Stephen A. Douglas. Once he and Lincoln had wanted to marry the same girl, Mary Todd from Kentucky. She married Lincoln.

Now the men were rivals again — political

rivals. In 1858 Lincoln ran against Douglas for Senator. They held debates in public all around the state of Illinois. Lincoln lost the election, but his debates with the famous Senator Douglas made Lincoln famous too. In 1860 the Republican Party, which opposed slavery, chose Lincoln to run for President. Stephen A. Douglas was the Democratic candidate that year.

This time Lincoln won. But victory brought him little joy. Between Election Day in

Frail, timid Clara Barton overcame her fears to become a nurse in the Civil War. Later she founded the American Red Cross.

November and Inauguration Day in March, seven Southern states separated from the Union. They feared Lincoln would end slavery as soon as he became President. Within six weeks after Lincoln took office, Southern soldiers fired on a U.S. fort in South Carolina. The Civil War had begun.

Sad, but determined, Abraham Lincoln led the fight to save the Union — and to end slavery. In 1863 he signed the Emancipation Proclamation, which said that slaves in the Confederate states would be "forever free." (Three years later the 13th Amendment to the Constitution ended slavery throughout the United States.)

Meanwhile many thousands of boys and men were dying in that terrible war. One of the last to fall was President Lincoln himself.

In the last days of the Civil War, just after his second term began, President Lincoln and his wife went to a play at Ford's Theater in Washington. While everyone was watching the stage, a man named John Wilkes Booth crept up behind the President and shot him in the head. Lincoln died the next day. Speaking for our sorrowing nation, a member of his Cabinet said, "Now he belongs to the ages."

Andrew Johnson

Born: December 29, 1808
Died: July 31, 1875
Years in office: April 15, 1865 — March 3, 1869
Party: Democratic

I t happened only once in our history. The President of the United States was on trial like a criminal.

His offense? Dismissing a Cabinet member without permission from Congress. The punishment? If two thirds of the U.S. Senators found him guilty, he could no longer be President. It would mean a terrible end to the career of a man who had worked his way up from the very bottom.

Andrew Johnson's parents were so poor that he couldn't even go to school. They sent their son to be a tailor's helper for seven years, but Andrew ran away. He felt he had learned enough to be a tailor, so he opened his own shop in Greeneville, Tennessee. When he was 18, Andrew married Eliza McCardle. She was only 16. She read to him while he sewed, and taught him how to write.

Soon the tailor shop was a meeting place for young workingmen. Andrew was their leader. At 22 he became mayor of the town. Later he went to Congress.

When the Civil War broke out, every South-

We paid Russia $7,200,000 for Alaska in 1867. That was a bargain — but considered so foolish at the time it was called "Seward's Icebox." (Secretary of State Seward arranged the deal.)

erner in the U.S. Senate quit and went home — all but Andrew Johnson. President Lincoln admired this Southerner who hated slavery and loved the Union. When Lincoln ran for his second term, he chose Johnson to run as his Vice President. Then suddenly Lincoln was dead and Johnson was President.

The Civil War was over. What should be done about the South? Congress wanted to punish the Southerners as rebels and traitors. President Johnson wanted to forgive those who promised to be loyal to the Union.

Edwin Stanton, the Secretary of War, sided with Congress. Johnson fired Stanton from the Cabinet, but Congress said he had no right to do this. Congress impeached Johnson — that is, called him to trial.

After the trial, which Johnson refused to attend, the Senate voted 35 to 19 against him. If one more Senator had voted "guilty," Johnson would have been removed.

Congress has never again impeached a President.

Ulysses Simpson Grant

Born: April 27, 1822
Died: July 23, 1885
Years in office: March 4, 1869 — March 3, 1877
Party: Republican

In the Mexican War, during the battle of Monterrey, some American soldiers found themselves almost out of ammunition. A young lieutenant volunteered to ride through the Mexican lines. He leaped on his horse, clung to its side with only one leg in the saddle, and raced through the enemy's bullets to get help for his men.

That daring lieutenant, Ulysses S. Grant, rode horses like a champion, but he hated war and army life.

Grant quit the Army and tried farming. He also tried selling land. In both these jobs he lost money. Finally his father gave him a job in the family's leather store. "Lyss" Grant was now 39 years old, and everyone thought he was a failure.

Then came the Civil War, and Grant became leader of some volunteer soldiers from Illinois. In the East, the war was going badly for the Union side. Soon people began hearing about Grant's victories in the West. President Lincoln put him in command of all the Union Armies, and Grant led the North to victory.

With the Civil War over, and Lincoln dead,

Builders of the first cross-country railroad met in Utah on May 10, 1869. They drove a gold spike into the last piece of track.

U. S. Grant was the most famous man in the country. It seemed the natural thing to elect him President. But in the White House, Grant lost much of the nation's respect. He put unworthy friends in office, who cheated and stole.

After his term ended, his personal troubles continued. He started a business, but his partner was dishonest. The business failed and Grant lost all his money — and other people's money too.

Grant wanted to pay off his debts. He hoped to earn the money by writing his life story. His friend Mark Twain promised to get the book published.

So Grant started dictating the book. When he developed cancer of the throat and could not speak any more, he wrote out his thoughts by hand.

It was a good book and sold very well. (You can still buy it.) It made his family rich, but Grant never knew that. Four days after he wrote the last word, he died.

Rutherford Birchard Hayes

Born: October 4, 1822
Died: January 17, 1893
Years in office: March 4, 1877 — March 3, 1881
Party: Republican

Duty was always calling to Rutherford Birchard Hayes. He did all he could to improve things around him — especially schools, prisons, and hospitals. Hayes was one of our most serious Presidents.

His wife Lucy was just as earnest as he was. As First Lady, Mrs. Hayes was called "Lemonade Lucy" because she never served any liquor in the White House. She didn't allow dances or card parties there either. The Hayes family (they had eight children) said their prayers together every morning and sang hymns every evening.

That doesn't mean the White House was a solemn place. Far from it! The Hayes family loved company, and they often filled the reception room with extra cots and couches for overnight visitors. If all the beds were full, their son Webb slept in the attic on an old billiard table. (It was stored away because the Hayeses didn't approve of games like billiards.) Sometimes the house was so overrun with guests, the President locked himself in the bathroom to get his work done.

In 1877, one of the very first models of a new invention — the telephone — was installed in the White House. The inventor, Alexander Graham Bell, was on hand to give the President a personal demonstration.

After the election of 1876, nearly everyone — even Hayes himself — thought that he had lost to Samuel J. Tilden, the Democratic candidate. But some Republicans claimed that Hayes had carried three Southern states which had been counted for Tilden. A committee of Congress was set up to investigate. They decided that Hayes, not Tilden, had been elected President.

President Hayes promptly did something to cheer up the angry Democrats. He withdrew all of the U.S. soldiers who had been serving as "occupation troops" in the South since the end of the Civil War. The Southern states could then handle their own affairs without any interference from the North. Ever since then, Democrats have run the state governments in most Southern states.

James Abram Garfield

Born: November 19, 1831
Died: September 19, 1881
Years in office: March 4, 1881 — Sept. 19, 1881
Party: Republican

The last President to be born in a log cabin was James Abram Garfield. He grew up on a farm in Orange, Ohio.

When he was 16, James worked for a while as a bargeman on a nearby canal, leading the mules that pulled the boats. Then he went to school to become a teacher of Latin and Greek. James was left-handed, but he could write with either hand. He liked to amaze people by writing Greek with one hand and Latin with the other — at the same time!

He became interested in politics, but the Civil War interrupted his ambitions. He was a good soldier, and at age 30 became the youngest general in the Union Army.

Later, Garfield served for 18 years in the

U.S. Congress, and in 1880 he was chosen to be the next U.S. Senator from Ohio. Then a surprising thing happened to Garfield. Before he had a chance to serve as Senator, he was elected President!

How did this happen?

The Republicans could not decide on a candidate for President in 1880. They voted 35 times

In the early 1880's cowboys herded thousands of Texas cattle north, to be shipped by railroad. Then farmers began putting up barbed wire fences, and the great cattle drives were over.

without agreeing. On the next try, they chose Garfield. Garfield was delighted at his unexpected nomination — and even more delighted when he won!

President Garfield was known to be kind-hearted, and many men came to him asking for government jobs. It was not possible for him to say yes to all of them. Among those he had to disappoint was a man named Charles Guiteau. One day Guiteau followed the President to a railroad station and shot him.

Garfield's death from the wound two months later made the nation realize that job-seekers were not only annoying to a President, but also dangerous. We began to look for a better way of filling government jobs. The next President helped find the way.

Chester Alan Arthur

Born: October 5, 1830
Died: November 18, 1886
Years in office: Sept. 20, 1881 — March 3, 1885
Party: Republican

Many good citizens were dismayed when Vice President Chester Alan Arthur became President. They feared he was unfit for the job and would do whatever the political bosses told him to do. They needn't have worried. The new President surprised everyone with his honesty and courage.

At first, everything about Arthur suggested he would be a weak leader. This wealthy lawyer liked rich, easy living. He had a French cook and a valet to serve him. He dressed elegantly in the latest styles. When he became President, he wouldn't even move into the White House until it had been fixed over to suit his fancy tastes. To make way for expensive new furniture, 24 wagonloads of old things were carted away.

71

People were suspicious of Arthur for another reason, too. Once President Rutherford Hayes had fired him from an important position. Like many politicians of his time, Arthur would hand out government jobs to his own friends and political followers. Hayes disapproved of this. He

In the 1880's steamships brought a million people a year from Europe to new homes in America. These immigrants crowded into our growing cities and found work in our growing industries.

thought government jobs should be earned by proven ability, not given as favors.

Arthur and Hayes seemed to disagree. Yet as President, Arthur changed. To everyone's surprise, he demanded the same thing Hayes had wanted — a fair system of filling government jobs. Arthur took an important step toward that goal. He persuaded Congress to pass the nation's first civil service law. This law said that people had to pass tests in order to get certain kinds of government jobs. Today there are civil service exams for almost all government jobs.

Many politicians were angry with President Arthur because now they had fewer jobs to give away in exchange for favors. As a result, his party would not consider Arthur as their candidate in the next election. President Arthur's courage cost him his career, but it won him the respect of the people.

Grover Cleveland

Born: March 18, 1837
Died: June 24, 1908
Years in office: March 4, 1885 — March 3, 1889
March 4, 1893 — March 3, 1897
Party: Democratic

G rover Cleveland's father was a preacher. He
taught his son always to be honest. Little
Grover would rock his baby sister's cradle, sing-
ing, " 'Tis a sin to steal a pin...."

Much later, as sheriff of Erie County, New
York, Grover Cleveland exposed many dishonest
men. People respected him so much that in 1882
they elected him mayor of the large city of Buffalo. Within a year he was elected governor of
New York. The year after that he was elected
President of the United States.

Cleveland was the only President to have
his wedding inside the White House. His bride,
Frances Folsom, was 22 years old — 27 years

younger than he was. She made a home for him in the White House — his first real home since he had left his family at the age of 16 to earn a living.

Cleveland is the only President who served two completely separate terms. After Cleveland's first term, Benjamin Harrison became President. But Mrs. Cleveland told the White

Large labor unions were formed as industry expanded. In 1894 President Cleveland proclaimed Labor Day as a public holiday.

House staff, "I want to see everything just as it is now when we come back." And four years later they really did come back. Cleveland had been elected President again.

These four years were not as happy as the first four. The country suffered a terrible business depression, and millions of people were out of work. Then came a personal shock. Doctors told the President he had cancer of the jaw.

Cleveland feared the country would be even more troubled if the people knew about his illness. So he met his doctors for a secret operation aboard a yacht in New York Harbor. The operation was a success, and nobody knew about it until years afterward.

For a long time Cleveland's two separate terms caused confusion in counting Presidents. Should he be counted as one President or two? Finally the State Department settled the question. They said he would be listed as both the 22nd and 24th Presidents, with Benjamin Harrison in between.

Benjamin Harrison

Born: August 20, 1833
Died: March 13, 1901
Years in office: March 4, 1889 — March 3, 1893
Party: Republican

Benjamin Harrison was born into a political family. His father was a Congressman from Ohio. His grandfather was "Old Tippecanoe" Harrison, the ninth President of the United States. And his great-grandfather — for whom he was named — was one of the men who signed the Declaration of Independence.

When he was 20 years old, and already a lawyer, young Ben Harrison married his boyhood sweetheart, Caroline Scott. They settled down in Indianapolis, Indiana. There he practiced law and began to be active in politics.

Harrison was respected by people but not really well liked. He seemed cold and unfriendly. He sometimes wore gloves to protect himself

Most of the first cars were run by steam or electricity. Then the Duryea brothers built the first U.S. gasoline-powered auto.

from other people's germs — and that just wasn't very neighborly!

After one term as a U.S. Senator, Harrison was not re-elected. He came home to Indiana saying he was a "dead duck" in politics. Yet the very next year, in 1888, the Republicans nominated him for President. His opponent Grover Cleveland was very popular, but Harrison won.

As President, Harrison let Congress run the country. It was the first Congress to spend more than a billion dollars in peacetime.

Life in the White House was extremely orderly while the Harrisons were there. Breakfast was always at eight, followed by a half hour of family prayers. Lunch was always at one. Supper was early, and so was bedtime.

During President Harrison's term, the White House was wired for electricity. The Harrisons were so afraid of getting shocks from the switches that they sometimes left the lights burning all night until someone came to turn them off.

While they were still in the White House, Mrs. Harrison died, and her niece, Mary Dimmick, took over as hostess. Later, Harrison married Mary. Their daughter Elizabeth was born 43 years after Harrison's first son, Russell.

William McKinley

Born: January 29, 1843
Died: September 14, 1901
Years in office: March 4, 1897 — Sept. 14, 1901
Party: Republican

T he 23rd Ohio Volunteers went into action at
daybreak in the bloody battle of Antietam,
during the Civil War. A few hours later, a wagon
came bumping up to the front lines. Such deli-
cious smells! Eighteen-year-old William McKinley, the driver, jumped down and began dishing
out hot food to the weary men.

"From his hands every man in the regiment
was served with hot coffee and warm meats, a
thing that had never occurred under similar cir-
cumstances in any other army in the world,"
McKinley's commander said later.

McKinley was made an officer for his bravery at Antietam. And his thoughtfulness for the
men that morning was as typical of him as his

courage. This considerate, kindly man became one of our best-loved Presidents.

His kindness showed in his devotion to Mrs. McKinley, who was often ill. A sickness caused her to faint at the most unexpected moments — even at banquets and public meetings. The President was always at her side to watch over her.

McKinley's great popularity helped him win the Presidency twice against William Jennings

Typewriters made new jobs for women in offices. Till then, they worked chiefly as factory workers, servants, or teachers.

Bryan, a young and famous speechmaker. Bryan was the favorite of the nation's farmers. Many farmers were in debt and blamed the men who supported McKinley — the bankers, manufacturers, and merchants of our fast-growing cities. But McKinley promised prosperous times and "a full dinner pail" for all. And in fact, during his time as President, business was good and jobs were easy to get.

President McKinley's second term ended in tragedy. One day he stood shaking hands with people in Buffalo, New York. A man with a bandage on one hand came along the line. Hidden under the bandage was a gun. The man fired twice, and McKinley fell, wounded. Eight days later he died.

Theodore Roosevelt

Born: October 27, 1858
Died: January 6, 1919
Years in office: Sept. 14, 1901 — March 3, 1909
Party: Republican

Theodore Roosevelt was such a sickly child that he could not go to school. He was thin, weak, jumpy, and so nearsighted that he kept bumping into things. Not a good start for the man who became our most vigorous President!

Luckily his father was wealthy enough to construct a gymnasium inside their New York City home. There young Teddy Roosevelt punched away at a punching bag, twirled Indian clubs, and swung on horizontal bars. Gradually he built up his weak body.

In college he became a boxer. Later he went to the North Dakota Bad Lands and worked as a cowboy. Once a gunman in a bar poked fun at Teddy because of his glasses. "Four-eyes is going to treat!" roared the gunman. "Four-eyes" knocked the man to the floor and took away his guns.

Orville and Wilbur Wright, two bicycle mechanics from Ohio, built the first heavier-than-air machine that flew by its own power.

Later, Roosevelt returned to New York City. As head of the police, he would roam around the city at night to see for himself that the laws were being carried out.

President McKinley made him Assistant Secretary of the Navy. Then the Spanish-American War broke out. Roosevelt wanted to fight. He quit his government job and organized a regiment of volunteer soldiers called "Rough Riders." He led his men in a charge up a hill in Cuba and became a hero.

Afterward, as governor of New York, he fought hard against crooked politicians. Many leaders of his own party were worried. Where would he strike next? One of them had an idea: They would be safer if Roosevelt could become Vice President. At that time a Vice President did not have much influence in government affairs.

When McKinley won a second term in 1900, Roosevelt was elected as his Vice President. Suddenly, McKinley was shot. At 42, Theodore Roosevelt became our youngest President.

"T.R." ran the Presidency just as strenuously as he did everything else. He arranged for the digging of the Panama Canal. He "busted trusts." The "trusts" were big companies in such industries as coal, steel, oil, and railroading. "T.R." believed they might become so powerful that they would control the government. So he saw to it that some of the trusts were broken up.

In the White House, Roosevelt's six energetic children made news. The younger ones walked on stilts over the White House floors, slid down bannisters, and took their pony upstairs in the elevator.

Roosevelt was elected to serve another term. When it ended, he was just 50 years old. Now he had time for travel and for the hunting he enjoyed so much.

But he was restless. It was hard for Roosevelt to be just a former President. In 1912 he decided to run for President again. However, the Republicans nominated William Howard Taft. So "T.R." organized a brand-new political party, known as the "Bull Moose" Party. Once, while Roosevelt was on his way to make a campaign speech, a man shot him. Roosevelt went right ahead and made his speech with the bullet in his chest. Afterward he went to the hospital and recovered quickly from the wound.

He lost that election. But many of his ideas, such as protecting the nation's forests, were carried out. While he was President, Theodore Roosevelt added more than 125 million acres to the national forest system. He was one of the first Presidents to recognize that we must begin to conserve our natural resources.

Roosevelt's last adventure began when he heard of an unexplored river in the jungles of Brazil, known as the River of Doubt. He decided to explore it. "You'll be lucky to come back alive," his friends said, and they were right. For two months he rode down the river's swirling rapids until at last, sick and injured, he came to a settlement. Brazil renamed the river "Rio Teodoro," or Theodore River.

Theodore Roosevelt always looked ahead. He felt that each day brought something new and exciting. Even the unknown did not frighten him. Just before he died he said, "Life and death are parts of the same great adventure."

William Howard Taft

Born: September 15, 1857
Died: March 8, 1930
Years in office: March 4, 1909 — March 3, 1913
Party: Republican

Many boys dream of becoming President. Not William Howard Taft! He wanted to be a judge, like his father and his grandfather.

Taft did become a judge, in his home state of Ohio, when he was 30 years old. But that was only the first of many important jobs. In the years ahead he was to work under three Presidents.

Taft was appointed a judge by President Benjamin Harrison. Then President McKinley needed him. McKinley was looking for a man to help set up a government in the Philippine Islands, our new territory which we had gained in the Spanish-American War. McKinley picked Taft. The next President, Theodore Roosevelt, was so pleased with Taft's work that he made him governor of the Philippines.

Roosevelt called Taft "the most loveable personality I have ever known." In 1908 Roosevelt insisted that the Republicans nominate Taft for President. And Taft won.

President Taft lived up to that word "loveable." In the White House he was jolly and fun-

The frame of a Model T Ford started at one end of the factory. Each worker added parts. The finished car rolled out the other end of the factory. It was the first auto assembly line (1913).

loving. Even though he was large, he was a fast tennis player and a graceful dancer. When the baseball season of 1910 opened, President Taft was invited to toss out the first ball. Thus he started one custom that all Presidents after him have followed.

Meanwhile Theodore Roosevelt was keeping an interested eye on his friend Taft. It seemed to him that President Taft was giving businessmen too many favors. Roosevelt quarreled with Taft, and by 1912 he and Taft had actually become enemies. Both men ran for President that year. Both lost — to Woodrow Wilson, the Democratic candidate.

A new and happier career lay ahead for Taft. He became a professor of law. Then in 1921 he was once more named a judge — this time of the highest court in the land. He was named Chief Justice of the United States.

Woodrow Wilson

Born: December 28, 1856
Died: February 3, 1924
Years in office: March 4, 1913 — March 3, 1921
Party: Democratic

Woodrow Wilson didn't go to school at all until he was 13 years old. He was taught at home by his father. But he went to college longer than any President — until he was 29. After he was graduated from one college, he went on studying and received two more diplomas.

Wilson became a professor of history. At Princeton University, he was the most popular teacher. He was strict with the students, but he knew how to have fun too. He loved to watch sports, and was always in the stands cheering when Princeton teams played. Among friends he would crack jokes, dance, and sing, in a beautiful voice.

Later Wilson became president of Princeton University. In 1910, Democratic leaders in New

Jersey were looking for a nice respectable candidate for governor of the state. They wanted an inexperienced person who would follow their orders. Wilson seemed like just the man.

How wrong they were! As governor, Wilson began at once to clean up the government in New Jersey. He put through laws to get rid of crooks in business and politics. He was so successful that in 1912 the Democrats nominated him for President. He won the election over Taft, the Republican, and Roosevelt, the "Bull Moose" candidate.

In the White House, Wilson kept up his work

By 1919 women could vote in 15 states. The 19th Amendment to the Constitution in 1920 gave them the right to vote nationally.

for good government. Under his leadership, Congress cut the taxes on imported goods, started the income tax, helped farmers borrow money more easily, shortened the working day for railroad men, and made important new laws to control big businesses.

But trouble was on the way. World War I had started in Europe. At first President Wilson said America should stay out of the war. He said America was "too proud to fight." When he ran for President again in 1916, Wilson reminded the nation that he had "kept us out of war."

Just one month after his new term began, the war came closer. German submarines sank some U.S. ships. Now Wilson said that America

Pitcher George Herman Ruth was a baseball hero. The "Babe" became the most exciting home-run hitter of all time.

must fight Germany. He hoped it would be "a war to end war."

Even while President Wilson called for war, he was planning for the time when there would be peace again. He had his plan ready when World War I ended. It included a "League of Nations." The "League" would be a meeting place where all nations could settle their quarrels without any more war.

The League of Nations was set up. Many nations joined, but not the United States. Wilson was disappointed and bitter, but more determined than ever to get us to join. He made a long speaking trip to try to convince Americans that the United States should join the League. During this trip he became very ill, and never fully recovered.

In the last year of his term, President Wilson was an invalid. He depended very much on the help of his wife, Edith. She was his nurse, secretary, and constant companion.

Without America as a member, the League of Nations never grew strong enough to keep peace in the world. Yet as Wilson himself said, "Ideas live; men die." Out of his idea for a League of Nations came the great world organization we have today: the United Nations.

Warren Gamaliel Harding

Born: November 2, 1865
Died: August 2, 1923
Years in Office: March 4, 1921 — August 2, 1923
Party: Republican

"I don't expect to be the best President, but I hope to be the best-loved one," said Warren G. Harding. Instead, he became a disappointed President.

Harding was a tall, handsome, friendly fellow. Back home in Marion, Ohio, he blew a horn in the local band, played first base on the ball team, and was especially good at poker.

His first love was newspaper work. When he was 19 years old, he and two friends borrowed 300 dollars and bought the town's weekly paper. Harding did everything from selling ads to running the presses. The paper became a success and soon was published every day.

As a successful newspaperman, Harding got to know Ohio's political bosses. They helped him become lieutenant governor of Ohio and, later, a U.S. Senator. Then in 1920 the Republicans nominated Harding for President.

In his campaign, Harding made up a catchy new word — "normalcy." Harding said that life in America had been upset by World War I. He promised the people that he could bring the nation "back to normalcy." The voters liked that idea, and gave Harding seven million more votes than they gave his opponent.

At the start, everything went smoothly for the new President. The nation seemed to go back

Radio came to American homes in the 1920's. You listened with a headset. It was hard to hear, but it was exciting anyway.

to normal as he had promised. Then the people started hearing suspicious stories about a U.S. Navy oil field out West, called "Teapot Dome." Some of Harding's advisers in the Cabinet had turned the rich Teapot Dome oil fields over to their personal friends.

A tremendous scandal broke out. One Cabinet member went to jail for taking bribes. Other officials were accused of stealing government money. Harding's closest advisers had betrayed him.

Disappointed and worried, Harding set out on a speech-making tour to try to explain things to the American people. During this trip he died suddenly of a stroke.

A few years ago some historians rated the Presidents, from the best to the poorest. As you might expect, Lincoln and Washington headed the list. At the bottom, as our "least successful" President, was Warren G. Harding.

Calvin Coolidge

Born: July 4, 1872
Died: January 5, 1933
Years in office: August 3, 1923 — March 3, 1929
Party: Republican

Vice President Calvin Coolidge was visiting on his father's farm in Vermont when President Harding died. Coolidge got up in the middle of the night to take the Oath of Office as President.

This sensible New Englander was just the man needed to end people's worry about the Harding scandals. Coolidge stood for the good old-fashioned ideas of honesty and thrift.

As a boy, he had done chores on the family farm — taking the cows to pasture, planting potatoes, driving the horses at harvest time, bringing in firewood for the kitchen stove. He gave his sons the same kind of upbringing. Once Calvin, Jr., had a job on a tobacco farm. Another worker said to him, "If my father were President,

Charles Lindbergh, "the Lone Eagle," became world-famous when he made the first solo flight across the Atlantic in 1927.

I wouldn't have to work." Calvin answered, "If my father were your father, you would!"

No other President was elected to so many different offices — from town councilman to governor. In 1919 the police in Boston, Massachusetts, went on strike. Governor Coolidge sent the Massachusetts State Guard to keep order. Coolidge declared: "There is no right to strike against the public safety by anybody, anywhere, at any time." This strong action made him well known all over the country. The next year he was elected Vice President.

After he became President, Coolidge was as careful and thrifty as ever. White House guests sometimes were served only plain ice water — in paper cups! "Cal" relaxed by fishing or by riding an electric horse that bucked him up and down. Nearly every night he was in bed by ten o'clock, and he took two-hour naps in the afternoons.

The voters decided to "keep cool with Coolidge," and they elected him President in 1924. Then in 1927 his party wanted him to be a candidate for President once more. He answered, "I do not choose to run for President in 1928." That's all he would ever say about it. He returned to his Massachusetts home, as popular as ever.

In the happy "Roaring Twenties," Americans went wild over a dance, the Charleston. Even members of Congress danced it in Washington.

Herbert Clark Hoover

Born: August 10, 1874
Died: October 20, 1964
Years in office: March 4, 1929 — March 3, 1933
Party: Republican

Americans seldom lived more gaily than in the years just before Herbert Hoover became President. The world was at peace. It was easy to get a job. People spent money as fast as they could make it — or faster.

Then, just a few months after Hoover's Inauguration, everything went wrong. Banks closed. Factories closed. Farmers couldn't sell their crops. The worst business depression in our history settled over the country.

Hoover kept hoping that better times were "just around the corner." Instead, the depression got worse and worse. By 1932, more than 12 million workers were out of jobs. Many people blamed Hoover. In the election for President that year, he lost by a huge number of votes.

For Hoover, those depression years were the unluckiest of his long lifetime — which included four separate careers.

Hoover was born poor. He studied to become a mining engineer. While he was still in his twenties, he discovered rich gold and coal fields in Australia and China. Soon he was a millionaire.

World War I brought him a second career.

The nation was panic-stricken when the stock market crash of 1929 started the worst business depression in our history.

He collected food for war refugees in Belgium and France. When the U.S. entered the war in 1917, Hoover took charge of our country's food supplies, too. Everyone learned to "hooverize" — to help win the war by saving food.

Hoover's fame as a good organizer and manager led him into his third career, as politician and President.

After he was President, Hoover found a fourth career, as adviser to Presidents who followed him. In World War II, he again helped to feed hungry victims of war. Later he served on important government committees.

Herbert Hoover died on October 20, 1964 — two months and ten days after he had celebrated his 90th birthday.

Franklin Delano Roosevelt

Born: January 30, 1882
Died: April 12, 1945
Years in office: March 4, 1933 — April 12, 1945
Party: Democratic

All over the nation people pulled their chairs closer to their radios to hear the new President. "This great nation will revive," said the mellow voice of Franklin Delano Roosevelt. "The only thing we have to fear is fear itself."

Americans everywhere felt a thrill of hope. They were going to fight the depression! They were going to win!

The smiling, vigorous President who led the fight looked as powerful as a boxer from the waist up. But from the waist down, he was paralyzed by polio. He dragged 60 pounds of leg braces around with him, and could not even stand without help.

Yet no one thought of Roosevelt as crippled. He was so active! Boldly he tried one experiment after another to get American business going again. He started a dozen or more brand-new government activities, including the National Recovery Administration and Tennessee Valley Authority. They were all known by their initials — "N.R.A.," "T.V.A." — and were jokingly called "alphabet soup." Some of these new plans worked, and some didn't. But the important thing was that more people had jobs and they felt more confident.

President Roosevelt called his program the "New Deal." He said it would help all America, but especially the "forgotten man" — the man who is poor and discouraged.

Gradually business improved. The better it got, the angrier some businessmen became with President Roosevelt. They said that "that man in the White House" was giving workers too many rights, and making it hard for owners of businesses to earn profits.

The working people loved Roosevelt. They elected him to a second term and a third term and a fourth term. No other President served so long. No other one will, for the 22nd Amendment to the Constitution says that no President may be elected more than twice.

Franklin Roosevelt was always doing new things. He was the first to go to a National Convention and accept the nomination for President in person. He was the first President to travel around by plane, the first to appear on TV, the first to appoint a woman to his Cabinet.

In Germany, the dictator Hitler threatened to attack the nearby countries. Roosevelt turned his attention more and more to the crisis overseas. Then, in 1939, World War II started in Europe. America joined the war in 1941.

Like President Wilson, President Roosevelt looked forward to winning the peace as well as winning the war. He said that America and her allies should stick together after the war to help keep peace. In this way, the United Nations began.

The United Nations was born as an alliance of nations in World War II. Its aim is to make sure there is no World War III.

During World War II the First Lady visited our troops fighting half way around the world in the Southwest Pacific.

"F. D. R." did not live to see the end of World War II. He died suddenly on April 12, 1945, while taking a few days' rest at his favorite vacation spot, the "little White House" in Warm Springs, Georgia.

Three families have given our nation two Presidents each — the Adamses, the Harrisons, and the Roosevelts. Franklin Roosevelt was only a distant cousin of Theodore Roosevelt, but he made the link closer by marrying Theodore's niece, Eleanor.

No First Lady in our history has been so argued about, so hated by some, or so loved by many. After her husband's death, she carried on his work for peace. Her work in the United Nations made her famous in every land. When she died in 1962, Eleanor Roosevelt was known as the "First Lady of the World."

Harry S. Truman

Born: May 8, 1884
Died: December 26, 1972
Years in office: April 12, 1945 — January 20, 1953
Party: Democratic

"I feel as though the moon and all the stars and all the planets have fallen upon me." That is what Vice President Harry Truman said when, at Franklin Roosevelt's death, he suddenly became President, in the midst of World War II.

President Truman was faced with an awesome decision. The mightiest weapon ever known, the atomic bomb, had been invented. Should America use it to stop the war? At Truman's order, one atomic bomb wiped out most of the big city of Hiroshima, Japan. Another did great damage to a second Japanese city, Nagasaki. Then Japan surrendered, ending World War II.

Now Truman worked to keep the peace. He

The first Atom bomb was exploded in the New Mexico desert on July 16, 1945. It was the beginning of a new era — the nuclear age.

helped the United Nations get started, and helped rebuild the war-damaged cities of Europe. Later, he sent American soldiers to stop an attack by Communist soldiers in South Korea.

Harry S. Truman (the "S" doesn't stand for anything) was a small-town boy from Missouri. When he couldn't go to West Point because of bad eyesight, he joined the Missouri National Guard. For a while he managed his father's farm.

In 1917, when the United States entered World War I, Lieutenant Truman went to France. He fought in some of the war's toughest battles, and was promoted to major. Home again, he ran a men's clothing store, but it failed.

Then Truman went into politics. He rose to become a U.S. Senator. His fine Senate record led the Democrats to nominate him for Vice President in 1944.

Theodore Roosevelt called his program the "Square Deal." Franklin Roosevelt had the "New Deal." President Truman said he wanted a "Fair Deal" for everyone. However, some businessmen thought the Fair Deal was unfair to them. These men didn't want Truman to be President a second time.

The experts said he would never get enough votes to be elected in 1948. But Truman was confident that he would. He traveled 30,000 miles and made 350 speeches to the American people. He fooled the experts and won the election.

The rooftops of America took on a new look as TV antennas began to sprout. At first a 10-inch screen seemed pretty big.

Dwight David Eisenhower

Born: October 14, 1890
Died: March 28, 1969
Years in office: Jan. 20, 1953 — Jan. 20, 1961
Party: Republican

Dwight David Eisenhower was nicknamed "Ike" by his boyhood pals. Even when he was President, people still spoke of him as "Ike." They didn't mean to be disrespectful. It was just the comfortable way they felt toward this friendly man with the big smile.

His name was David Dwight Eisenhower at first. When he got older, he switched the first two names around because he liked them better that way.

He was only two years old when his family moved from Texas to Abilene, Kansas, at the end of the Chisholm Trail. Abilene had been one of the wildest towns of the old Wild West. In the 1890's it was still a tough place for poor folks like the Eisenhowers to get along. They lived on the "south side" — in the rundown part of town. The six Eisenhower brothers stuck together in fist fights against "north side" boys.

"Ike" was Abilene High School's best football and baseball player. He went to West Point and made the football team there, too. But in his first season, a broken knee ended his football days. Later on he became a good golfer.

Young Eisenhower made only a fair record at West Point. After graduation, he entered the Army. He never got into battle in World War I.

The submarine *Nautilus*, first ship with an atomic engine, sailed 60,000 miles on a single load of atomic fuel.

When World War II broke out, he was a lieutenant colonel.

Then he moved up fast. Soon he was a four-star general, in command of all our military forces in Europe. He led the United States and our allies to victory over Germany.

General Eisenhower was now so popular that both political parties wanted him to be their candidate for President in 1948. He refused. But in 1952 he agreed to run — as a Republican. That year, and again in 1956, he defeated the Democratic candidate, Adlai Stevenson.

Though "Ike" had been a soldier, as President he worked hard for peace. He traveled thousands of miles on good-will tours to other lands.

Dwight Eisenhower was the first President to celebrate his 70th birthday in the White House. Soon after, he retired to his farm in Gettysburg, Pennsylvania.

John Fitzgerald Kennedy

Born: May 29, 1917
Died: November 22, 1963
Years in office: Jan. 20, 1961 — Nov. 22, 1963
Party: Democratic

All our previous Presidents looked like fathers or grandfathers. John Fitzgerald Kennedy looked like an older brother. He was tall and well built, and had a happy smile. He had trouble making his thick hair stay down.

People liked to see pictures of this youthful man and his good-looking family. Some even said that his handsome appearance was one of the things that made them want to vote for him.

John F. Kennedy's great-grandfather had come to this country from Ireland. John's grandfather was a leading politician in Boston, Massachusetts. John's father, Joseph P. Kennedy, served as a U.S. Ambassador to England for a time.

Joseph Kennedy's family lived in Mas-

The Mercury capsule carried America's first astronauts into space. The capsule glows as it re-enters earth's atmosphere.

sachusetts in a big home with many servants. But the nine Kennedy children were not spoiled. Each one had to make his own way as a person in life. John's way was to study extra hard. He was graduated with honors from Harvard College. While he was still in his twenties, he wrote a book that was published.

At first John did not plan to go into politics. His brother Joe was going to do that. Then Joe was killed in World War II, and John decided to take his place.

After serving in the war himself and winning a medal for bravery, John came home and was elected to Congress. In 1953 Senator Kennedy married Jacqueline Lee Bouvier. He wrote another book, *Profiles in Courage,* for which he won an important national award, the Pulitzer Prize. In 1960 the Democratic Party nominated him for President, and he won the election.

The new President was 43 years old, but he looked much younger. Some people were afraid at first that he didn't have enough experience. But "J.F.K." worked vigorously, and soon had the respect of people all over the world.

John F. Kennedy might have become one of our greatest Presidents. We will never know. On November 22, 1963, as the President rode in an open car in a parade in Dallas, Texas, a man hiding along the parade route shot him. A few minutes later, President Kennedy was dead.

Lyndon Baines Johnson

Born: August 27, 1908
Died: January 22, 1973
Years in office: November 22, 1963 — January 20, 1969
Party: Democratic

I n November, 1963, three letters became the best-known initials in the nation: L. B. J. They stood for:

Lyndon Baines Johnson, our 36th President, Lynda Bird Johnson and Luci Baines Johnson, his two lively daughters, and "Lady Bird" Johnson — the nickname of his wife Claudia.

Johnson had wanted to run for President in 1960. The Democrats nominated John Kennedy instead, so Johnson agreed to run for Vice President.

Then came the terrible day of November 22, 1963. Johnson was riding through Dallas, Texas, two cars behind the President. Shots rang out, and President Kennedy fell, fatally wounded.

That same day, on a plane ready to rush him back to Washington, Johnson took the Oath of Office as President. To Congress, the new President said, "Let us continue." Under Johnson's leadership, Congress passed the Civil Rights Bill, a cut in taxes, and other programs that Kennedy had fought for.

President Johnson had his own programs too. America, he said, could become a "Great Society" — a land where everyone could look forward to a good education, a comfortable and useful life, and an old age without worry.

In 1964 the voters gave a tremendous vic-

A Civil Rights Bill was begun by President Kennedy and signed by President Johnson. It reassured for all Americans the rights of citizenship that are guaranteed to us in the Constitution.

tory to the nation's new leader and his program. Nearly everyone expected the President to run for reelection in 1968, but Johnson astonished the world by announcing he was not a candidate. Why? The frustrating war in Vietnam — where half a million Americans were fighting — had split the nation. Many in Johnson's own party blamed him because the war dragged on and peace seemed far away. So he decided to step aside.

The Democrats, still not united, lost the election. Johnson and his Cabinet gave the new Republican President all the help they could to start him off in his big new job. Then Lyndon Johnson slipped away to the place he loved best — his ranch on the Pedernales River in Texas.

Richard Milhous Nixon

Born: January 9, 1913

Years in office: January 20, 1969 — August 9, 1974

Party: Republican

At 12 o'clock noon on August 9, 1974, President Richard M. Nixon left office, the first President ever to resign.

Nixon was born only a few miles from the Pacific Ocean in Yorba Linda, California. His ancestors were colonial settlers whose sons and grandsons kept moving west with the moving frontiers. He was graduated from Whittier College in California and Duke University Law School in North Carolina.

After serving in the U.S. Navy during World War II, Nixon returned home and was elected to Congress in 1946. In two short years (1951-53) he rose from Congressman to Senator to Vice President under Eisenhower. Then in 1960 the Democrats were back in power. But in 1968 their can-

Television took Americans onto the battlefields of Vietnam; the sights and sounds of the war were instantly relayed into millions of homes.

didate was defeated by Nixon. His reelection in 1972 was his greatest political success.

Two years later, the scandal of Watergate forced the President's resignation. "Watergate" began in June, 1972, when five men broke into the headquarters of the Democratic National Committee in the Watergate building in Washington.

It was soon discovered that the people responsible for the break-in were working for the Committee to Reelect the President. Over the next two years people close to the President in the White House tried to cover up this crime.

The Senate formed a committee to investigate the Watergate matter. At the end of their hearings it was likely that the Congress would vote to impeach the President. Nixon decided to resign. While he was flying back to his home in California, his Presidency ended.

Richard Nixon was the first American President in nearly 25 years to visit a communist country. In 1969 he traveled to Rumania. In 1972 he visited the People's Republic of China and the U.S.S.R. World peace was his highest hope. One of the most important events of his Presidency was to bring American combat troops home from Vietnam. The long, costly war in Vietnam had seriously divided the country. When at last the troops were coming home, Nixon reached the height of his popularity.

A private, withdrawn man, Richard Nixon had fought hard to become President. Watergate, serious inflation, and the forced resignation of his own Vice President, Spiro T. Agnew, all overshadowed his real achievements on the international scene.

Gerald Rudolph Ford

Born: July 14, 1913

Years in office: August 9, 1974 – January 20, 1977

Party: Republican

For the first time in our history, a Vice-President not elected by the people became President.

Gerald Ford had been chosen by Richard Nixon to be Vice-President when Spiro Agnew resigned. The Senate and the House of Representatives approved the choice. When Richard Nixon left office, Gerald Ford moved into the White House.

A rugged-looking, athletic man, Gerald Ford seemed to be just the person who was needed to restore the country's faith in the Presidency. He was open, friendly, and promised to listen to the people.

Gerald Ford was a mid-Westerner. He was

born in Omaha, Nebraska, and raised in Grand Rapids, Michigan. During his high school and college years, Gerald Ford was a star football player, and could have played professional football. He was graduated from the University of Michigan and Yale University Law School.

In 1942, four months after the start of World War II, Gerald Ford joined the U.S. Navy. He served for 47 months in the Pacific. After he returned to Grand Rapids, he was elected to Congress and served there from 1948 on, until he was picked to be Vice-President.

Fuel shortages, inflation, and increasing unemployment were three big issues that brought some loss in President Ford's popularity. But America was also celebrating its 200th birthday. It was a time to look back at all that had been accomplished in our country — and to look forward to the future.

James Earl Carter

Born: October 1, 1924
Years in office: January 20, 1977–
Party: Democratic

Carter liked his nickname *Jimmy*, and spoke of himself as a "simple country boy." He had grown up in the small town of Plains, Georgia (population 550), and took over the family's peanut farm and business there when his father died. He was an active civic leader in his hometown, a school board member, and a deacon of the local church. He'd married a Georgia girl, Rosalynn Smith, and they had four children.

But the "simple country boy" had also graduated with honors from the U.S. Naval Academy, served in the Navy's nuclear submarine program, and studied nuclear physics. As a state senator he was voted a most effective legislator.

Jimmy Carter was governor of Georgia when he first decided to try for the Presidency, yet he was practically unknown outside the south. Traveling almost alone and carrying his own luggage, he criss-crossed the nation, campaigning for human rights and "competent and compassionate government." Flashing his wide smile, he promised, "I will never lie to you." That had strong appeal to Americans after Watergate.

At the Democratic national convention in 1976, Carter was nominated on the first ballot, and won a narrow victory over Republican Gerald Ford.

Carter took office with the well wishes of the nation. People warmed to his family, complete with grandmother (Miss Lillian). They liked it that nine-year-old Amy Carter attended public school, that Rosalynn was her husband's close adviser and co-worker, and that Carter jogged for exercise. And Carter's simple, sincere manner and ready smile invited the nation's cooperation.

But effective leadership was needed in the months ahead. The gas shortage, conflicts over nuclear energy, the rising cost of living, inflation, and troubles in the Middle East were among the country's pressing problems.

Carter played a key role in bringing about a

peace treaty between Israel and Egypt. But as Congress continued to delay many of his programs for energy, tax, health, and welfare reforms, the feeling grew that he was an uncertain leader.

Then Iranian students seized the U.S. Embassy in Iran and held Americans hostage, demanding the exiled Shah's return to stand trial. Americans were shocked and angry, and as weeks became months, freeing the hostages became one of the campaign issues of 1980.

Trouble at the Three Mile Island plant raised sharp questions about the safety of nuclear energy.

☆ ☆ **ELECTION SCORECARD** ☆ ☆

This is the year America votes for a President. You can keep your own election returns with this scorecard.

THE CANDIDATES' NAMES	NUMBER OF POPULAR VOTES	NUMBER OF ELECTORAL VOTES
Democratic *FOR PRESIDENT*	_____	_____
FOR VICE-PRESIDENT		
Republican *FOR PRESIDENT*	_____	_____
FOR VICE-PRESIDENT		
Other Candidates *FOR PRESIDENT*	_____	_____
FOR PRESIDENT	_____	_____

IN MY STATE

If elections have changed these names, enter in right-hand column.

_____ _____
GOVERNOR

_____ _____
U.S. SENATOR

_____ _____
U.S. SENATOR

_____ _____
Representative from my District